This Journal Belongs To

_____

BY EVER JOURNALS

Bismillah

Salam & congratulations for taking this step in investing your time in coming closer to Allah.

Insha'Allah this is the beginning of a new journey in which you fall in love with the words of Allah every day.

So why take up Qur'an journaling?
Well, just like in any other type of learning, taking notes by hand enhances the learning experience and increases the chance of retaining information.
As Qur'an journaling will be an important type of learning you will do, retaining the information you discover is paramount.

This Qur'an Journal not only provides you with a template to structure your learning but gives you a beautiful keepsake that you can look through whenever you want and even pass on to your children Insha'Allah.

What you will need...

- ☐ A source of Tafseer-this can be a book or an online resource
- ☐ Your favourite writing tool
- ☐ A copy of the Qur'an in Arabic
- ☐ A copy of the Qur'an in translation

How to use the journal

Firstly you will need to set the intention that you are doing this to please Allah and become closer to Him. You will only get what you intend, so make your intention now.

Secondly, you'll need to decide on a time of day to journal. What day will you journal? Every day or once a week? Be realistic so that you can keep to the habit.

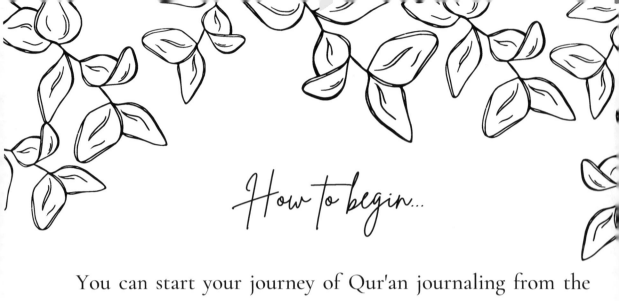

How to begin...

You can start your journey of Qur'an journaling from the beginning, by starting at surah Fatiha and working your way down. Alternatively, you can start with the easier and shorter surahs and work your way up. Or you can even choose a surah that you personally love and find yourself reciting all the time. The choice is yours.

This journal comes with a Qur'an tracker so you can tick off the surahs as you go. Be sure to use it as a visual representation of your success, as it will keep you motivated to keep going.

Once you've decided on where to begin, start by writing out the chosen ayah in Arabic. If you find this part very difficult you can print it out and stick it in the Ayah box. Then using your Quran translation, write out the basic translation of that ayah.

Use the 'Key words' box to jot down words that you think are essential to this ayah, or write any new vocabulary that you want to learn.

Think about the theme that has come up in the translation. Write it down in the specified box.

After that, you can refer to your tafseer sources to write out the explanation of the ayah. You can use more than one tafseer source if you wish to do so. You'll find that you may have more to add to the key themes and vocabulary box after studying the tafseer. That's ok, go back and add to your notes.

The Qur'an is not just a book, but a guide on how to live. So it's essential you put to work the gems that you learn.
This is why I've provided you with a 'My reflections' box where you can add your thoughts, make connections to other ayahs and reflect on what you've learnt. Following that, go ahead and make an action plan.

How can you implement what you've learnt into your daily life?
What new habits can you build?
What behaviour will you avoid?
Is there a dua you want to learn?

There will certainly be ayahs where no action is required, and that's ok, you can leave that box blank.
The most important thing is to try and implement what you learn.

I pray that this Qur'an Journal fulfils its role in helping you to strengthen your connection with Allah's words.
I pray that Allah accepts your efforts and mine.

Salam & happy journaling.

Qur'an Journaling Tracker

☐	1.Al-Fatiha	☐	19.Mariam
☐	2.Al-Baqarah	☐	20.Ta-Ha
☐	3.Ali-Imran	☐	21.Al-Anbiya
☐	4.An-Nisa	☐	22.Al-Hajj
☐	5.Al-Maidah	☐	23.Al-Mu'minun
☐	6.Al-Anam	☐	24.An-Nur
☐	7.Al-A'raf	☐	25.Al-Furqan
☐	8.Al-Anfal	☐	26. Ash-Shu'ara
☐	9.At-Tawbah	☐	27. An-Naml
☐	10.Jonah	☐	28. Al-Qasas
☐	11.Hud	☐	29. Al-Ankabut
☐	12.Yusuf	☐	30. Ar-Rum
☐	13.Ar-Ra'd	☐	31. Luqman
☐	14.Ibrahim	☐	32. As- Sajdah
☐	15.Al-Hijr	☐	33. Al-Ahzab
☐	16. An Nahl	☐	34. Saba
☐	17.Al-Isra	☐	35. Fatir
☐	18.Al-Kahf	☐	36. Ya-Sin

Qur'an Journaling Tracker

☐ 37. As- Saffat	☐ 55. Ar-Rahman
☐ 38. Sad	☐ 56. Al-Waqi'ah
☐ 39. Az-Zumar	☐ 57. Al-Hadid
☐ 40. Ghafir	☐ 58. Al- Mujadilah
☐ 41. Fussilat	☐ 59. Al-Hashr
☐ 42. Ash-Shura	☐ 60. Al-Mumtahanah
☐ 43. Az-Zukhruf	☐ 61. As-Saff
☐ 44. Ad-Dukhan	☐ 62. Al-Jumu'ah
☐ 45. Al-Jathiyah	☐ 63. Al-Munafiqun
☐ 46. A-Ahqaf	☐ 64. At-Taghabun
☐ 47. Muhammed	☐ 65. At-Talaq
☐ 48. Al-Fath	☐ 66. At-Tahrim
☐ 49. Al-Hujurat	☐ 67. Al-Mulk
☐ 50. Qaf	☐ 68. Al-Qalam
☐ 51. Az-Zariyat	☐ 69. Al-Haqqah
☐ 52. At-Tur	☐ 70. Al-Ma'arij
☐ 53. An-Najm	☐ 71. Nuh
☐ 54. Al- Qamar	☐ 72. Al-Jinn

Qur'an Journaling Tracker

- [ ] 73. Al-Muzzammil
- [ ] 74. Al-Muddaththir
- [ ] 75. Al-Qiyamah
- [ ] 76. Al-Insan
- [ ] 77. Al-Mursalat
- [ ] 78. An-Naba
- [ ] 79. An-Nazi'at
- [ ] 80. Abasa
- [ ] 81. At-Takwir
- [ ] 82. Al-Infitar
- [ ] 83. Al-Mutaffifin
- [ ] 84. Al-Inshiqaq
- [ ] 85. Al-Buruj
- [ ] 86. At-Tariq
- [ ] 87. Al-A'la
- [ ] 88. Al-Ghashiyah
- [ ] 89. Al-Fajr
- [ ] 90. Al-Balad

- [ ] 91. Ash-Shams
- [ ] 92. Al-Layl
- [ ] 93. Ad-Duha
- [ ] 94. Ash-Sharh
- [ ] 95. At-Tin
- [ ] 96. Al-Alaq
- [ ] 97. Al-Qadr
- [ ] 98. Al-Bayyinah
- [ ] 99. Az-Zalzalah
- [ ] 100. Al- Adiyat
- [ ] 101. Al-Qari'ah
- [ ] 102. At-Takathur
- [ ] 103. Al-Asr
- [ ] 104. Al-Humazah
- [ ] 105. Al-Fil
- [ ] 106. Quraysh
- [ ] 107. Al-Ma'un
- [ ] 108. Al-Kawthar

Qur'an Journaling Tracker

- [ ] 109. Al-Kafirun
- [ ] 110. An-Nasr
- [ ] 111. Al-Masad
- [ ] 112. Al-Iklas
- [ ] 113. Al-Falaq
- [ ] 114. An-Nas

"My Lord,
increase me in knowledge."

- Quran 20:114

DATE: | M T W T F S S

Surah: Ayah:

Translation

Key vocabulary   Main theme / related verses

Tafseer

My reflections

Action plan

DATE: | M T W T F S S

Surah: Ayah:

Translation

Key vocabulary   Main theme / related verses

Tafseer

My reflections

Action plan

DATE: | M T W T F S S

Surah: Ayah:

Translation

Key vocabulary   Main theme / related verses

Tafseer

My reflections

Action plan

DATE: | M T W T F S S

Surah: Ayah:

Translation

Key vocabulary   Main theme / related verses

Tafseer

My reflections

Action plan

DATE: | M T W T F S S

Surah: Ayah:

Translation

Key vocabulary   Main theme / related verses

Tafseer

My reflections

Action plan

DATE: | M T W T F S S

Surah: Ayah:

Translation

Key vocabulary

Main theme / related verses

Tafseer

My reflections

Action plan

DATE: | M T W T F S S

Surah: Ayah:

Translation

Key vocabulary   Main theme / related verses

Tafseer

My reflections

Action plan

DATE: M   T   W   T   F   S   S

Surah: Ayah:

Translation

Key vocabulary   *Main theme / related verses*

Tafseer

My reflections

Action plan

DATE: | M T W T F S S

Surah: *Ayah:*

Translation

Key vocabulary   *Main theme / related verses*

Tafseer

My reflections

Action plan

DATE: | M T W T F S S

Surah: Ayah:

Translation

Key vocabulary   Main theme / related verses

Tafseer

My reflections

Action plan

DATE: | M T W T F S S

Surah: Ayah:

Translation

Key vocabulary   Main theme / related verses

Tafseer

My reflections

Action plan

DATE: | M T W T F S S

Surah: Ayah:

Translation

Key vocabulary Main theme / related verses

Tafseer

My reflections

Action plan

DATE: | M T W T F S S

Surah: Ayah:

Translation

Key vocabulary   Main theme / related verses

Tafseer

My reflections

Action plan

DATE: | M T W T F S S

Surah: Ayah:

Translation

Key vocabulary Main theme / related verses

Tafseer

My reflections

Action plan

"All humans are dead except those who have knowledge, and all those who have knowledge are asleep, except those who do good deeds, and those who do good deeds are deceived, except those who are sincere, and those who are sincere are always in a state of worry."

—Imam Shafi'i

DATE: | M T W T F S S

Surah: Ayah:

Translation

Key vocabulary

Main theme / related verses

Tafseer

My reflections

Action plan

DATE: | M T W T F S S

Surah: Ayah:

Translation

Key vocabulary   Main theme / related verses

Tafseer

My reflections

Action plan

DATE: M T W T F S S

Surah: Ayah:

Translation

Key vocabulary   Main theme / related verses

Tafseer

My reflections

Action plan

DATE: | M T W T F S S

Surah: Ayah:

Translation

Key vocabulary   Main theme / related verses

Tafseer

My reflections

Action plan

DATE: M T W T F S S

Surah: Ayah:

Translation

Key vocabulary   Main theme / related verses

Tafseer

My reflections

Action plan

DATE: | M   T   W   T   F   S   S

Surah:

Ayah:

Translation

Key vocabulary

Main theme / related verses

Tafseer

My reflections

Action plan

DATE: | M T W T F S S

Surah:

Ayah:

Translation

Key vocabulary

Main theme / related verses

Tafseer

My reflections

Action plan

DATE: | M T W T F S S

Surah: Ayah:

Translation

Key vocabulary   Main theme / related verses

Tafseer

My reflections

Action plan

DATE: | M T W T F S S

Surah: Ayah:

Translation

Key vocabulary   Main theme / related verses

Tafseer

My reflections

Action plan

DATE: | M T W T F S S

Surah: Ayah:

Translation

Key vocabulary   Main theme / related verses

Tafseer

My reflections

Action plan

DATE: | M T W T F S S

Surah: Ayah:

Translation

Key vocabulary   Main theme / related verses

Tafseer

My reflections

Action plan

DATE: | M T W T F S S

Surah: Ayah:

Translation

Key vocabulary   Main theme / related verses

Tafseer

My reflections

Action plan

DATE: | M T W T F S S

Surah: Ayah:

Translation

Key vocabulary   Main theme / related verses

Tafseer

My reflections

Action plan

DATE: | M T W T F S S

Surah:

Ayah:

Translation

Key vocabulary

Main theme / related verses

Tafseer

My reflections

Action plan

DATE: | M T W T F S S

Surah: Ayah:

Translation

Key vocabulary   Main theme / related verses

Tafseer

My reflections

Action plan

Surah: Ayah:

Translation

Key vocabulary   Main theme / related verses

Tafseer

My reflections

Action plan

DATE: | M T W T F S S

Surah: Ayah:

Translation

Key vocabulary   Main theme / related verses

Tafseer

My reflections

Action plan

DATE: | M T W T F S S

Surah: *Ayah:*

Translation

Key vocabulary   *Main theme / related verses*

Tatseer

My reflections

Action plan

DATE: | M T W T F S S

Surah: Ayah:

Translation

Key vocabulary   Main theme / related verses

Tafseer

My reflections

Action plan

DATE: M   T   W   T   F   S   S

Surah: *Ayah:*

Translation

Key vocabulary

Main theme / related verses

Tafseer

My reflections

Action plan

"Knowledge from which no benefit is derived is like a treasure out of which nothing is spent in the cause of God."

– Al-Tirmidhi

DATE: | M T W T F S S

Surah: _____ Ayah: _____

Translation

Key vocabulary

Main theme / related verses

Tafseer

My reflections

Action plan

DATE: | M T W T F S S

Surah: Ayah:

Translation

Key vocabulary   Main theme / related verses

Tafseer

My reflections

Action plan

DATE: | M T W T F S S

Surah: Ayah:

Translation

Key vocabulary

Main theme / related verses

Tafseer

My reflections

Action plan

DATE: | M   T   W   T   F   S   S

Surah: Ayah:

Translation

Key vocabulary   Main theme / related verses

Tafseer

My reflections

Action plan

DATE: M T W T F S S

Surah: _____ Ayah: _____

Translation

Key vocabulary

Main theme / related verses

Tafseer

My reflections

Action plan

DATE: | M T W T F S S

Surah: *Ayah:*

Translation

Key vocabulary   *Main theme / related verses*

Tafseer

My reflections

Action plan

DATE: M   T   W   T   F   S   S

Surah: Ayah:

Translation

Key vocabulary   Main theme / related verses

Tafseer

My reflections

Action plan

DATE: | M T W T F S S

Surah: Ayah:

Translation

Key vocabulary   Main theme / related verses

Tafseer

My reflections

Action plan

DATE: | M T W T F S S

Surah: Ayah:

Translation

Key vocabulary   Main theme / related verses

Tafseer

My reflections

Action plan

DATE: M T W T F S S

Surah: Ayah:

Translation

Key vocabulary   Main theme / related verses

Tafseer

My reflections

Action plan

DATE: | M T W T F S S

Surah: Ayah:

Translation

Key vocabulary   Main theme / related verses

Tafseer

My reflections

Action plan

DATE: M T W T F S S

Surah: Ayah:

Translation

Key vocabulary

Main theme / related verses

Tafseer

My reflections

Action plan

DATE: | M T W T F S S

Surah: Ayah:

Translation

Key vocabulary   Main theme / related verses

Tafseer

My reflections

Action plan

DATE: | M T W T F S S

Surah: *Ayah:*

Translation

Key vocabulary   *Main theme / related verses*

Tafseer

My reflections

Action plan

DATE: | M T W T F S S

Surah: Ayah:

Translation

Key vocabulary   Main theme / related verses

Tafseer

My reflections

Action plan

"Studying is bitter,
but remaining ignorant is infinitely
more bitter."

- Shaykh Yasir Qadhi

DATE: M T W T F S S

Surah: Ayah:

Translation

Key vocabulary   Main theme / related verses

Tafseer

My reflections

Action plan

DATE: | M   T   W   T   F   S   S

Surah: *Ayah:*

Translation

Key vocabulary

Main theme / related verses

Tafseer

My reflections

Action plan

DATE: | M T W T F S S

Surah: Ayah:

Translation

Key vocabulary Main theme / related verses

Tafseer

My reflections

Action plan

DATE: | M T W T F S S

Surah: Ayah:

Translation

Key vocabulary   Main theme / related verses

Tafseer

My reflections

Action plan

DATE: | M T W T F S S

Surah: Ayah:

Translation

Key vocabulary   Main theme / related verses

Tafseer

My reflections

Action plan

DATE: | M T W T F S S

Surah: Ayah:

Translation

Key vocabulary   Main theme / related verses

Tafseer

My reflections

Action plan

DATE: | M T W T F S S

Surah: Ayah:

Translation

Key vocabulary   Main theme / related verses

Tafseer

My reflections

Action plan

DATE: M T W T F S S

Surah: Ayah:

Translation

Key vocabulary

Main theme / related verses

Tafseer

My reflections

Action plan

DATE: M T W T F S S

Surah: Ayah:

Translation

Key vocabulary   Main theme / related verses

Tafseer

My reflections

Action plan

DATE: | M   T   W   T   F   S   S

Surah: Ayah:

Translation

Key vocabulary   Main theme / related verses

Tafseer

My reflections

Action plan

DATE: | M T W T F S S

Surah: Ayah:

Translation

Key vocabulary   Main theme / related verses

Tafseer

My reflections

Action plan

DATE: | M T W T F S S

Surah: Ayah:

Translation

Key vocabulary

Main theme / related verses

Tafseer

My reflections

Action plan

DATE: | M T W T F S S

Surah: Ayah:

Translation

Key vocabulary Main theme / related verses

Tafseer

My reflections

Action plan

DATE: | M T W T F S S

Surah: Ayah:

Translation

Key vocabulary

Main theme / related verses

Tafseer

My reflections

Action plan

DATE: | M T W T F S S

Surah: Ayah:

Translation

Key vocabulary

Main theme / related verses

Tafseer

My reflections

Action plan

DATE: | M T W T F S S

Surah: Ayah:

Translation

Key vocabulary   Main theme / related verses

Tafseer

My reflections

Action plan

DATE: | M T W T F S S

Surah: Ayah:

Translation

Key vocabulary Main theme / related verses

Tafseer

My reflections

Action plan

DATE: | M T W T F S S

Surah: Ayah:

Translation

Key vocabulary   Main theme / related verses

Tafseer

My reflections

Action plan

DATE: | M T W T F S S

Surah: Ayah:

Translation

Key vocabulary   Main theme / related verses

Tafseer

My reflections

Action plan

DATE: | M T W T F S S

Surah: Ayah:

Translation

Key vocabulary   Main theme / related verses

Tafseer

My reflections

Action plan

DATE: M T W T F S S

Surah: *Ayah:*

Translation

Key vocabulary

Main theme / related verses

Tafseer

My reflections

Action plan

DATE: | M T W T F S S

Surah: Ayah:

Translation

Key vocabulary   Main theme / related verses

Tafseer

My reflections

Action plan

DATE: | M T W T F S S

Surah: *Ayah:*

Translation

Key vocabulary

Main theme / related verses

Tafseer

My reflections

Action plan

DATE: M T W T F S S

Surah: Ayah:

Translation

Key vocabulary

Main theme / related verses

Tafseer

My reflections

Action plan

DATE: | M T W T F S S

Surah: Ayah:

Translation

Key vocabulary

Main theme / related verses

Tafseer

My reflections

Action plan

DATE: M T W T F S S

Surah: *Ayah:*

Translation

Key vocabulary

Main theme / related verses

Tafseer

My reflections

Action plan

DATE: | M T W T F S S

Surah: *Ayah:*

Translation

Key vocabulary   *Main theme / related verses*

Tafseer

My reflections

Action plan

DATE: M T W T F S S

Surah:

Ayah:

Translation

Key vocabulary

Main theme / related verses

Tafseer

My reflections

Action plan

DATE: M T W T F S S

Surah: Ayah:

Translation

Key vocabulary   Main theme / related verses

Tafseer

My reflections

Action plan

DATE: M T W T F S S

Surah: Ayah:

Translation

Key vocabulary   Main theme / related verses

Tafseer

My reflections

Action plan

DATE: | M T W T F S S

Surah: *Ayah:*

Translation

Key vocabulary

Main theme / related verses

Tafseer

My reflections

Action plan

DATE: M T W T F S S

Surah: Ayah:

Translation

Key vocabulary

Main theme / related verses

Tafseer

My reflections

Action plan

DATE: M   T   W   T   F   S   S

Surah: Ayah:

Translation

Key vocabulary

Main theme / related verses

Tafseer

My reflections

Action plan

DATE: | M T W T F S S

Surah: Ayah:

Translation

Key vocabulary

Main theme / related verses

Tafseer

My reflections

Action plan

DATE: | M   T   W   T   F   S   S

Surah: *Ayah:*

Translation

Key vocabulary

Main theme / related verses

Tafseer

My reflections

Action plan

DATE: | M T W T F S S

Surah: *Ayah:*

Translation

Key vocabulary   *Main theme / related verses*

"I never argued with anyone with the intention to win, rather my intention was to seek the truth."

-Imam ash-Shafi'i

Tafseer

My reflections

Action plan

DATE: | M   T   W   T   F   S   S

Surah: *Ayah:*

Translation

Key vocabulary   *Main theme / related verses*

Tafseer

My reflections

Action plan

DATE: M T W T F S S

Surah: Ayah:

Translation

Key vocabulary   Main theme / related verses

Tafseer

My reflections

Action plan

DATE: | M T W T F S S

Surah: Ayah:

Translation

Key vocabulary   Main theme / related verses

Tafseer

My reflections

Action plan

DATE: M T W T F S S

Surah: *Ayah:*

Translation

Key vocabulary

Main theme/ related verses

Tafseer

My reflections

Action plan

DATE: M T W T F S S

Surah: Ayah:

Translation

Key vocabulary   Main theme / related verses

Tafseer

My reflections

Action plan

DATE: M T W T F S S

Surah: Ayah:

Translation

Key vocabulary

Main theme / related verses

Tafseer

My reflections

Action plan

DATE: M T W T F S S

Surah: Ayah:

Translation

Key vocabulary Main theme / related verses

Tafseer

My reflections

Action plan

DATE: | M T W T F S S

Surah: Ayah:

Translation

Key vocabulary   Main theme / related verses

Tafseer

My reflections

Action plan

DATE: M T W T F S S

Surah: *Ayah:*

Translation

Key vocabulary

Main theme / related verses

Tafseer

My reflections

Action plan

DATE: M T W T F S S

Surah: Ayah:

Translation

Key vocabulary   Main theme / related verses

Tafseer

My reflections

Action plan

DATE: M   T   W   T   F   S   S

Surah: Ayah:

Translation

Key vocabulary   Main theme / related verses

Tafseer

My reflections

Action plan

DATE: M   T   W   T   F   S   S

Surah: *Ayah:*

Translation

Key vocabulary

Main theme / related verses

Tafseer

My reflections

Action plan

"It is not the knowledge that
should come to you,
it is you who should come to the
knowledge."

-Imam Malik ibn Anas

DATE: | M   T   W   T   F   S   S

Surah: Ayah:

Translation

Key vocabulary   Main theme / related verses

Tafseer

My reflections

Action plan

DATE: | M T W T F S S

Surah:

Ayah:

Translation

Key vocabulary

Main theme / related verses

Tafseer

My reflections

Action plan

DATE: M   T   W   T   F   S   S

Surah:

Ayah:

Translation

Key vocabulary

Main theme / related verses

Tafseer

My reflections

Action plan

DATE: M T W T F S S

Surah: Ayah:

Translation

Key vocabulary

Main theme / related verses

Tafseer

My reflections

Action plan

DATE: M T W T F S S

Surah: Ayah:

Translation

Key vocabulary   Main theme / related verses

Tafseer

My reflections

Action plan

DATE: | M T W T F S S

Surah: Ayah:

Translation

Key vocabulary   Main theme / related verses

Tafseer

My reflections

Action plan

DATE: | M T W T F S S

Surah: Ayah:

Translation

Key vocabulary   Main theme / related verses

Tafseer

My reflections

Action plan

DATE: | M T W T F S S

Surah:

Ayah:

Translation

Key vocabulary

Main theme / related verses

Tafseer

My reflections

Action plan

DATE: M T W T F S S

Surah: Ayah:

Translation

Key vocabulary   Main theme / related verses

Tafseer

My reflections

Action plan

DATE: | M T W T F S S

Surah: Ayah:

Translation

Key vocabulary   Main theme / related verses

Tafseer

My reflections

Action plan

DATE: M   T   W   T   F   S   S

Surah: Ayah:

Translation

Key vocabulary   Main theme / related verses

Tafseer

My reflections

Action plan

DATE: M   T   W   T   F   S   S

Surah: Ayah:

Translation

Key vocabulary   Main theme / related verses

Tafseer

My reflections

Action plan

DATE: | M T W T F S S

Surah: Ayah:

Translation

Key vocabulary   Main theme / related verses

Tafseer

My reflections

Action plan

DATE: | M T W T F S S

Surah: Ayah:

Translation

Key vocabulary

Main theme / related verses

Tafseer

My reflections

Action plan

DATE: | M T W T F S S

Surah: Ayah:

Translation

Key vocabulary   Main theme / related verses

Tafseer

My reflections

Action plan

DATE: | M T W T F S S

Surah: Ayah:

Translation

Key vocabulary   Main theme / related verses

Tafseer

My reflections

Action plan

DATE: | M T W T F S S

Surah: *Ayah:*

Translation

Key vocabulary   *Main theme / related verses*

Tafseer

My reflections

Action plan

DATE: M T W T F S S

Surah: Ayah:

Translation

Key vocabulary

Main theme / related verses

Tafseer

My reflections

Action plan

DATE: | M T W T F S S

Surah: *Ayah:*

Translation

Key vocabulary   *Main theme / related verses*

Tafseer

My reflections

Action plan

DATE: | M T W T F S S

Surah: Ayah:

Translation

Key vocabulary   Main theme / related verses

Tafseer

My reflections

Action plan

DATE: | M T W T F S S

Surah: Ayah:

Translation

Key vocabulary   Main theme / related verses

Tafseer

My reflections

Action plan

DATE: M T W T F S S

Surah: *Ayah:*

Translation

Key vocabulary   *Main theme / related verses*

Tafseer

My reflections

Action plan

DATE: | M T W T F S S

Surah: Ayah:

Translation

Key vocabulary

Main theme / related verses

Tafseer

My reflections

Action plan

DATE: | M T W T F S S

Surah: *Ayah:*

Translation

Key vocabulary

Main theme / related verses

Tafseer

My reflections

Action plan

DATE: M   T   W   T   F   S   S

Surah: *Ayah:*

Translation

Key vocabulary   *Main theme / related verses*

Tafseer

My reflections

Action plan

DATE: M T W T F S S

Surah: Ayah:

Translation

Key vocabulary

Main theme / related verses

Tafseer

My reflections

Action plan

DATE: | M T W T F S S

Surah: *Ayah:*

Translation

Key vocabulary   *Main theme / related verses*

Tafseer

My reflections

Action plan

DATE: | M T W T F S S

Surah: Ayah:

Translation

Key vocabulary

Main theme / related verses

Tafseer

My reflections

Action plan

DATE: M   T   W   T   F   S   S

Surah:

Ayah:

Translation

Key vocabulary

Main theme / related verses

Tafseer

My reflections

Action plan

DATE: M   T   W   T   F   S   S

Surah: Ayah:

Translation

Key vocabulary   Main theme / related verses

Tafseer

My reflections

Action plan

DATE: M T W T F S S

Surah:

Ayah:

Translation

Key vocabulary

Main theme / related verses

Tafseer

My reflections

Action plan

DATE: M T W T F S S

Surah: Ayah:

Translation

Key vocabulary   Main theme / related verses

Tafseer

My reflections

Action plan

DATE: M   T   W   T   F   S   S

Surah:

Ayah:

Translation

Key vocabulary

Main theme / related verses

Tafseer

My reflections

Action plan

DATE: | M T W T F S S

Surah: *Ayah:*

Translation

Key vocabulary   *Main theme / related verses*

Tafseer

My reflections

Action plan

DATE: M   T   W   T   F   S   S

Surah: Ayah:

Translation

Key vocabulary

Main theme / related verses

Tafseer

My reflections

Action plan

DATE: | M T W T F S S

Surah: *Ayah:*

Translation

Key vocabulary   *Main theme / related verses*

"Whoever desires this world must seek its knowledge, and whoever desires the next world, must seek its knowledge."

- Shaykh Yasir Qadhi

Tafseer

My reflections

Action plan

DATE: | M T W T F S S

Surah: *Ayah:*

Translation

Key vocabulary   *Main theme / related verses*

Tafseer

My reflections

Action plan

DATE: | M T W T F S S

Surah: Ayah:

Translation

Key vocabulary Main theme / related verses

Tafseer

My reflections

Action plan

DATE: | M T W T F S S

Surah: Ayah:

Translation

Key vocabulary   Main theme / related verses

Tafseer

My reflections

Action plan

DATE: | M T W T F S S

Surah: Ayah:

Translation

Key vocabulary   Main theme / related verses

Tafseer

My reflections

Action plan

Printed in Great Britain
by Amazon

36300733R00165